The Sur~ ~~~~h
Ques~

by Peter William Depp
Illustrated by Jennifer Fitchwell

Editorial Offices: Glenview, Illinois • Parsippany, New Jersey • New York, New York
Sales Offices: Needham, Massachusetts • Duluth, Georgia • Glenview, Illinois
Coppell, Texas • Sacramento, California • Mesa, Arizona

flower

David and Emma love summers.
They stay on Grandma's farm.
They walk among the flowers and trees.
One day they find some seeds.
"What are these?" asks David.

seeds

"They are sunflower seeds,"
says Grandma.
"Where do they come from?"
asks Emma.
"They come from sunflowers," says
Grandma. "The flowers make the seeds."

3

Grandma shows them the sunflowers.
The tall flowers are yellow and brown.
"Shall we leave the seeds?" asks David.
"Let's plant them instead,"
says Grandma.

soil

Emma and David fill a box with soil.
Grandma helps them plant the seeds.
They water the seeds.
They wait.

David and Emma look in the box
every day.
After about ten days, they see
tiny stems.
They see tiny leaves among the stems.
"But where are the flowers?"
asks Emma.

"The plants must grow big,"
says Grandma.
"When summer ends, you will
see flowers."
"I have another question," says David.
"Will the flowers have seeds?"

"The seeds will be inside the sunflower,"
says Grandma.
"Seeds make flowers."
Emma says, "And flowers make seeds!"
David and Emma are very happy.
They know the answers to the sunflower
questions.